QUICK GUIDE TO MAXIMIZING YOUR PAST EXPERIENCES FOR YOUR PRESENT MOMENT

I0418084

TRANSFORMATION
TO
GREATNESS

FRANCKY L. JEANTY

ISBN:

979-8-9874492-1-9

ACKNOWLEDGEMENTS

I would like to acknowledge and give my warmest thanks to my Aunt
Ysmelia Valliere who made this work possible. Her guidance and advice
carried me through all the stages of my life. Because of her, I was able to
transform into the man that I am today.

*I would also like to express my appreciation and gratitude to the following special people
who made a big impact in my life:*
My wonderful parents who have giving me the golden opportunity by
bringing to America; they have sacrificed their dreams and hopes in order
for me to achieve mine.

My Big brother Wilkens Valliere who always believe in me no matter what.
Without him, I could never have undertaken this journey. Thank you so
much for not giving up on me.

My nephew Benoit Charles who has helped me through this journey of
mine. Thank you for keeping me up to date on my social media platform.
He continues to motivate me every day and for that, I am grateful.

My friend Nickson Nixon Christopher for encouraging me every step of
the way through this process. Without his support, this endeavor would
have not been possible.

*I would like to express my special thanks of gratitude to the following people for their
guidance and support throughout my journey:*
Dr Lonnie Morris, Dr Edward Alexander, Dr Benjamine Okafor, Dr,
Rubens Perichie, Dr Judith Scott, and John Webber. Thank you all
for shaping me into the person that I am today.

I would also like to extend my gratitude to Grayson Marshall for being in
inspiration in my life and also for providing me with all the tools and
guidance that I need to continue with my journey.

Special thanks to Rackhouse Publishing team, specifically "Melynda
Rackley" for her hard work and guidance.

"In America you can become anything you want to become. You simply have to change your mindset and refine the person you are now in the present moment, and then you will see the best version of yourself."
-Francky L Jeanty

TRANSFORMATION TO GREATNESS

Contents

1
THE POWER OF ONE

What if I told you that all it takes is one person, one second, and one thought, to change your life? Would you believe me? I know it sounds like a fairy tale, but I know all too well how true it really is, as I have experienced it firsthand. This book is all about identifying your window of opportunity and making a conscious effort to transform your life. It hasn't been easy for me and it may not be easy for you, but it's possible even if it's hard.

Within each page I share pieces of my story in hopes that it will help you to embark on your own life transformation to greatness. While writing this book I experienced a moment of sadness as I retold the stories of my childhood. In those moments I had to find the good and acknowledge the role they played in becoming great. Of course, it wasn't an easy task and it's most certainly an ongoing one but it's necessary. Transformation requires us to look at the ugly truths of life and use them as fuel to achieve our next level of greatness. Just like me you have all the keys to your transformation within you. The first step to unlocking your greatness door is to become comfortable with the past and all the lessons that have come with your pain!

My story began like many immigrants, but I was determined to do everything in my power to maximize the opportunities given to me along the way. I was born in La Gonâve Island located just off the coast of Haiti. The population today is around 120,000 and it's still known for being a place for the poorest of the poor. Many of the occupants are uneducated because of the lack of access to education. Less than thirty percent of students enrolling in school make it to the sixth grade, and only twenty percent make it through middle school. This is partly because of the cost related to education. It wasn't deemed important enough to change the cost or access for all by the time I was born in 1983. My parents didn't complete high school and were very young at the time of my birth. I believe my mother desired to care for me and give me a better life but that came with challenges that a fourteen-year-old couldn't handle alone. My father wasn't much older than her and they both decided it would be best if I was raised by my father's sister when I was just a year old.

When I look at this now, I realize this was possibly one of the hardest decisions my mother had to make in her young teen years. I don't know why or how this decision came about but I believe it was vital to my development. She gave me the opportunity to experience living in a two-parent home within a community where I could sleep peacefully every night. She also, unknowingly, planted a seed within me to build and grow the courage to make difficult choices. In that way, I suppose I wanted to be brave like her. I don't imagine it being any easier for my father either since it was his sister who took me in. When I look back at this part of my life, I see how a man is responsible for making things happen. He knew they couldn't take care of me so the next best option was to find someone he trusted that could.

He planted seeds of resourcefulness and responsibility within me.

My aunt lived in Petit-Goâve, Haiti. This was also known as the countryside. The population is only around 12,000 and is known for being one of the oldest cities in the country. While it was a bit better than where I was born it was still riddled with poverty. I lived with my aunt, her husband and my cousin. We lived in a four-bedroom house but we were still poor and at times we struggled to pay the basic bills. I was eventually given the job of working out in the field because there wasn't enough money for my education. At times she seemed cruel and made sure I felt the pain that came with having another mouth to feed. It felt like there wasn't enough love in her home for me, so I obeyed her rules and tried my best to stay out of trouble.

In retrospect, it couldn't have been easy for my aunt to have more responsibilities and to her credit she made sure I had all of the necessities of life. Her demeanor was usually focused, serious and militant. There was no slacking in her house and if there was something that needed to be done, she ensured its completion. That's what made her great in my eyes, she never stopped until the task was done. It's what also made her tough. As a parent now, I see the importance of what she modeled with her tenacity, but I also see the need for gentleness and love when raising a child. I believe my aunt did the best she could based on what she knew with her limited education.

While I didn't enjoy the punishments and verbal threats

I can look back and realize she taught me the importance of time. She would spit on the ground and tell me to do a task and it had better be done before the spit dried. If the task wasn't done, a beating would be my end result. This taught me to move with urgency and stay focused but as a kid it felt like a burden too big for my small shoulders. Despite the lack of love I felt at home, I had other family members to talk to, which made me feel like someone cared.

I was around five or six years old when I found out that my aunt wasn't my birth mother. I don't remember which family member revealed the truth about my parents, but that one conversation was helpful to me. At first, I felt an unexplainable sadness and relief at the same time. I was sad because I couldn't understand why someone would give up their child. Then I was relieved because I thought that maybe one day they would come back to get me. Knowing this information caused so many questions to arise in my mind like how they chose my aunt to take care of me and when they planned to come back. I knew my aunt would never answer them so I never bothered to ask. The feeling of relief comforted me the most during the most painful punishments because I knew this wasn't my mother and that what I was experiencing wasn't normal behavior from a mom. I often imagined what life would have been like if I were with my parents, but I snapped myself out of it each time. In my mind, I knew it was better to stay focused on the challenges of the present rather than the past choices made by my parents that I couldn't change.

Just like my parents, my aunt didn't finish high school but unlike them, she couldn't read. I didn't realize this until it was brought to my attention by one of the other children in the neighborhood. As a proud woman, she didn't go around asking for help and tried to disguise her lack of literacy; she even forced me to learn to read and sometimes I would try and read things for her. I thought it was a punishment, but now that I'm an adult, I see it was her way of showing she cares. She knew the importance of education even though she couldn't afford to pay for me to go to school. I was the youngest boy in the home and it would have been too much of a sacrifice for me and my cousin to have an education, so by default he was chosen over me. My cousin's tutor would come to the house and give him lessons but he showed very little interest at times. I wanted the knowledge so I would sneak around to listen so I could memorize the lessons myself. This choice eventually paid off in a big way.

One day the tutor noticed that I could recite the lesson but my cousin couldn't. My aunt also noticed this, and that's when she decided to invest in my education too. To cover the new expense she sold extra goods and fresh produce from her garden at the market. The cost for the entire year was twenty five US dollars and when I saw her pay for it I felt blessed and sad for her because I realized shortly after starting school that she truly

"In my mind, I knew it was better to stay focused on the challenges of the present rather than the past choices made by my parents that I couldn't change"

couldn't read. The memory still replays in my mind at times.

I was sitting on the floor in the main area of our house and she came over to pick up a book and began looking at it. I noticed almost instantly that she was holding the book upside down. After looking over the pages for a moment she handed it to me and asked me to read it to her. I flipped it right side up and began to read the pages to her aloud. After I finished one page she gave me a small smile and told me to keep learning. After that day I always kept a book, paper and a pencil with me. Nothing would stop me from learning.

All it took was one second of me deciding I was going to take control of my education, and then it took one second of my aunt seeing my motivation and the teacher noticing my initiative. That's how powerful we all are inside if we choose to be. I wish I could say that life immediately got better after I started learning at home with my cousin's tutor but there were still a few ups and downs along the way.

Tough times were upon us in Haiti and even walking down the street was risky. 1991 is a year I can never wipe from my mind. President Jean-Bertrand Aristide faced opposition from powerful leaders in the country and was forced into exile. This led to a military committee governing Haiti. For nearly three years the government, gangs, and thugs killed close to 4,000 Haitians. Many more escaped to the Dominican Republic and out of desperation risked emigration across open water. During this time dangerous men would threaten young boys with force and kidnap them to join the gang. Your age didn't matter and when you saw them coming you knew you had to hide or out run them. If you tried to escape and denied their offer to join their gang, you risked being killed. I would overhear my older cousins and even my aunt talking about the dangers, but they never told me exactly what was going on. One of my cousins was advised to dress as a girl to avoid being snatched up on the street. My heart raced almost every time I walked home from school alone. My first encounter was around eight years old as I was walking to my aunt's house from school. I could hear gunshots but when I looked around, no one was there. I knew this was their warning shot to let people know they were coming and they would grab any boys that ran. I glanced behind me and saw a car coming full speed my way. Sweat poured from my face as I tried not to scream out in fear of my life. The only thing I could do was go inside of the broken-down school bus that was a few feet away from me. I crawled into the front of it as the smoke from a fire burned next to the back of it. I nestled myself underneath the seat and didn't move because I knew the risk of being taken from my family by the gangsters. I don't remember how long I stayed in that bus and there was no cell phone or pay phone available for me to use to let my family know I was safe. Eventually I remember waking up in the pitch-black bus as sweat slid down my back and mosquitoes nipped at my exposed arms. That walk home was one of the scariest times in my life and one of the only times I recall seeing a look of joy when my aunt saw me walk through the door. We never talked about the details and the only thing she knew was I ran from the gang and hid until they were gone. That was enough for her to hug me and in a way that showed me she loved me even if she never said the words aloud.

Things were rough for a while in our area because of the gangs and kidnappings. At one point the safest thing my aunt could do was hide me and my male cousin in the bushes so the gangs wouldn't know we lived with her. One night she told us to quickly dress in the darkest clothing we owned and lay down on the ground between the baseboards and the bushes outside the house. As a young boy I was frightened because my aunt seemed to be afraid for us, and she had never displayed fear until this day. Her friends had sons, nephews and brothers who had been taken and I could hear her calling out to the god she believed in to save us. Her quick thinking saved our lives because shortly after she gave us instructions two men knocked on the door claiming to be police and looking for a male suspect. It was really the gang members boldly coming to snatch up any young boys. We slept in the bushes outside that night and awoke to my aunt's voice telling us we were safe to go inside. Every day was a gamble and if she hadn't taught us to think quickly and hide fast we would have become one of the lost children of the countryside.

The days were long and the dangers were immense for a while

but I knew I could make something of myself if I finished school. Things got a little better in 1994 when the USA stepped in which led to President Jean-Bertrand Aristide's return. When we were back to being able to peacefully walk down the street to go to school, I took advantage of my opportunity and excelled. Eventually I even passed my older cousin in grades because he was held back. It was important for me to keep going, and when I could I helped him learn too. There were times when I would explain lessons to him because he would understand it better from me. I didn't pretend to be the best but I knew he needed my help and I had the power to show him what came easy to me. I never imagined that I would have that same opportunity when I worked in the field watching him learn, but I also never quit hoping for the impossible. My relentless pursuit gave me the fuel to achieve my goal and work to help my cousin overcome his challenges too.

Everything in life starts with one thought, choice or action. This is why it's so important to stay focused and committed to your desires. When you believe in something, go after it. Do what you can to help your dream become a reality. I don't know what made me decide to sneak and listen to the lesson that day with my cousin's teacher, but I'm glad I did. I was afraid I would get caught. My heart raced and my palms were sweaty at the thought of the beating I could possibly receive for not being outside working. There are some risks worth taking, especially when it will make your life better. It was the one split second decision that helped me in unimaginable ways. I didn't doubt myself or my desires, I just took action. If you are at a crossroad at any time in your life and must choose between action and inaction I encourage you to always take action, especially if it will make you better!

At the age of twelve the longing for a father figure or brother that could guide me intensified. Sometimes I would dream about having someone who would show me the love I wished I'd received from my mother and father. I knew I had other siblings but we weren't close because we had different mothers and lived in different cities. My cousin was like the know it all news reporter and always knew all of the adults' business. So I would find out in passing who I was related to but I was too uncertain to ask or try to build a relationship with any of them. I had no idea how to form meaningful connections at that time in my life. The desires for a big brother or father figure lived in my mind and sometimes popped up against my will. I now know that it's okay to have desires, and it's okay to dream. Dreaming is like a phone call with our soul. Sometimes our dreams warn us and other times they help us to hope. For me, dreaming was all about hope. I hoped there was more to life than struggle, beatings and running from thugs in a gang. And I hoped that one day I would experience love that didn't hurt. It was as if the entire universe was listening in on my thoughts and nodded in agreement. I will never forget the year of 1995 when hope and reality gave me a life changing gift.

Getting a phone call was rare in my aunt's house. I had no friends who needed to call me on the phone so when she called me and held the phone in my direction I was confused. She covered the speaker while whispering, "It's your brother." My heart sank to the pit of my stomach and for a second I forgot how to breathe. She gave me a look that shook me out of my daze and I grabbed the phone.

"Hello?"

"Hi little brother, how are you doing?"

His voice was rich with knowledge and the deepness commanded my attention. " I ... I ....I . .am ok." He seemed to sense my nervousness and replied but this time the deepness was lathered in a tone that made me feel his care.

"I called to talk to you about something. I have already talked with our aunt about it and now I want to share it with you." It felt like he was taking forever to get to the point of the call and my nervousness continued to build with every tick of the clock. I listened as he continued,

"Our father has purchased a home in Port-au-Prince but he is moving to America. He has given me permission to get you and our cousin from our aunt and move you both here with me. I promised to take care of you both as if you were my sons."

The words seemed to ring in my head like a fire alarm but

12

there was no danger here. This was my way out, this was my ticket to a better education and no more working in the field. I don't think I ever replied to my brother that day on the phone. He didn't give me a date or time but the promise alone was enough. That night I went to bed and cried but this time it wasn't because of a beating. The tears I shed on this day would be a result of my happiness. Even if he never came, knowing that my father hadn't forgotten about me mattered. Hearing that my big brother was going to care of me like I was his own son mattered. Being allowed to hear his voice on the phone and dream of moving to Port-au-Prince mattered.

That one phone call mattered more than anything I had ever experienced in my life at that point.

"There are some risks worth taking, especially when it will make your life better."

2
MAXIMIZE THE MOMENT

I remember looking into the eyes of a man sitting on the sofa and feeling an instant connection. I'd seen him around only a few times before in my life before but I didn't know the connection we shared until this day. In the past I only saw him at important family events like a funeral or maybe once at a holiday gathering but he was older and I can't recall us ever exchanging more than a quick glance. On this day none of that mattered, he was my oldest brother and he came to the house that day with only one mission.

As I gathered my few belongings I felt the nervous excitement rise in my chest. It was a moment of hopefulness that I will never forget. He came to get me and my cousin and move us to my fathers house just as he had promised on the phone. As I walked out of my aunt's house I looked up to the sky and felt as if the heavens had opened up for me that day. I felt like she would be able to breathe a little easier knowing there was no fear of us being kidnapped in the capital.

On the drive to the capital city I studied the road with intensity because this was the path that led to me getting a better education and a better life. When I arrived in the new city, I could not help but think about the possibilities of a better future. As the capital of Haiti, Port-au-Prince offered many different opportunities for education. My brother was passionate about our education and made sure to enroll my cousin and me into school at his first opportunity. Eventually he shared with me that my father had been helping in the background all along and came up with the idea to get me from my aunt as soon as he could. This made me feel something inside for my father that I hadn't felt before because I thought he'd forgotten about me. My father moved to America in 1991 and kept in contact with my aunt and brother to get updates on me when he could. His move to America saved his life and ours in many ways. The cost of living in Haiti was much lower than America which meant that even as an immigrant he could take care of us and we'd have a higher chance at success. This information was like the icing on the cake when I moved.

My brother showed me love from the moment he helped us pack our belongings into the car. But it wasn't until I saw him sewing my school uniform by hand that I felt his love for me. I knew I owed it to him to maximize the gift of education that he was allowing me. Many people have said it before me and I am sure you probably have heard it said a thousand times. But the saying is true: "It's not how you start that's important, but how you finish." Seeing him at the sewing machine lit a fierce fire inside of me, which became the fuel to make me focus on my education and not let him down. It gave me hope that I could be something. I still remember the color of that uniform and those colors make me smile. It was a yellow shirt with a navy blue tie and matching pants. He even made sure I had all the supplies I needed and I anxiously kept checking my backpack as he sewed

"... I am sure you probably have heard it said a thousand times. But the saying is true: "It's not how you start that's important, but how you finish."

the uniform. That day my brother became my role model, father figure and inspiration, and I was going to make sure he was proud of me.

Things were different moving from the countryside to the capital with my brother. The first day of school arrived quickly, and I sat in the classroom full of strangers with my arms folded and my legs shaking. The nervous energy flowed through me and rested on my shoulders but I tried to stay positive. The teacher glanced in my direction and we made eye contact, and I knew she saw the look of confusion in my eyes. Up until this point I spoke mostly creole but at the school the primary language was French. Things seemed to move at a different pace in the room but I knew I had to quickly jump into the new rhythm and get the words into my mind. I knew very little French so it made me even more nervous when the teacher came over to talk to me. She came over and asked, "Why do you look so nervous?"

"I am not nervous." I managed to piece together a basic french reply but she didn't believe me.

"Yes, you are. Go to the board and we will help you learn." Her tone was assertive, yet gentle, and I obeyed the command without a second thought. When I arrived at the board in the front of the room she gave me a sentence to write. I quickly scribbled the sentence on the board and then returned to my seat. She stood at my chair and when I sat she said, "You are still nervous, go back and try it again." The next time I returned to my seat, she didn't make me go back to the board. It was a small victory but just enough to help me get through the day.

When my brother picked me up from school I could tell he wanted to know the details of my first day. He waited until we arrived home after the bus ride before he asked, "So, how was school?" I didn't want him to think I was ungrateful so I carefully chose my words. "The school is very strict but I think I will like it with time."

He wasted no time with his reply, "Well if you want to make it at this school you have to study harder than the other students and you will have to get better with your French." I spoke a little of both languages with my aunt but not to the same degree so I understood what he was saying and nodded in agreement as he spoke. From that day forward he made it his business to help me with my French and eventually he even got me a tutor. There were moments when I felt overwhelmed bouncing from one language to another but each time I looked at my uniform I kept going. My brother loved me and believed I was worth staying up late to sew a uniform for. He made sure that every dime my father sent was used as it should be and even picked up odd jobs to make sure we could pay for a tutor plus school fees while going to school full time. I helped my cousin when I could, but he didn't seem to take it seriously. After a certain point I knew I had to let him find his own path. I needed to maximize every moment because this was an opportunity to make me better.

My aunt visited my cousin and I often after we moved to the capital and she seemed different. It was as if I had a whole new version of herself because she was much more caring when she visited, bringing us things from back home in the countryside. I began to truly see in my heart that it wasn't torture when I was living with her, she was really doing her best to raise disciplined men who knew the value of hard work. Her lessons helped me at the new school because I didn't waste time like some of my classmates. To top it all off, my brother took his role seriously because he knew the dangers of living in the capital. My cousin and I weren't allowed to go many places outside of school so my main goal was to learn.

My brother became my best friend, my only friend, my mentor and my role model. My brother was still very young when we went to live with him. Although he had exceptional skills he hadn't yet finished high school and he kept me close to him. We all left the house together and he made sure we got to our school on his own way there. At the end of the day he was always waiting at the gates to walk us home. Wherever he went I followed close behind, sometimes against my will. I didn't mind much because I knew he loved me and wanted to keep me off the streets. He taught me a lesson in maximizing the moment I will never forget. He rode a bicycle everywhere he went and they had a competition once.

The principal and one of the top teachers at his school

doubted him because he was from the country and an area that wasn't known for being smart or athletic. They joked and laughed at his desire to participate in the bike race but my brother knew he could do it and he made up his mind that he was going to win. There were twenty participants but when race day arrived he shook my hand and said, "Brother, I am going to be number one!" I stood in amazement as he walked over to the teacher and the principal who laughed at him and said, "If I can't be number one I will be number two but I will not quit." He won the race that day and that entire year everyone saw him excel and achieve every academic goal or challenge he set his mind to.

He went on to graduate high school and college and he kept his word to watch over us. There wasn't much fun going on in the house and his friends were just as serious as he was. One of the only places we did go was to his friend Gilbert's house, he also had siblings my age so at first I was excited when my brother told me this. The excitement quickly faded when we arrived at the quiet house. Curiosity got the best of me and I couldn't help but ask, "Where is everyone"?

Gilbert spoke sternly saying, "They are all studying. I can show you into the room with my little brother and you can study with him."

I didn't want to spend my evening studying but there were no other options so I sat quietly in the room with the stranger and stared at the words on the page. Everytime we went to visit

Gilbert they were always doing homework or studying. Eventually I was allowed to talk with my father on the phone and I remember him telling me to surround myself with people I wanted to be like, who could help me. It was clear that he had taught my brother the same things because we were surrounded by people who wanted the best education Haiti could offer.

Even with the knowledge that education would take me places I needed to have fun. I wanted to get out and make friends. I knew my brother wouldn't approve of purposeless outings but I also knew he would allow me to play sports with the goal of getting a scholarship for college. I presented the idea and shortly after, I started playing soccer. The chances of me getting a soccer scholarship were slim so my main motive was to have something to do after school besides go home and study. My brother would fuss at me for going over to the field to play soccer because we played rough. As a kid I didn't care that we didn't have medical insurance and if something happened to me that my brother would struggle to get me care. Those worries were beyond me at the time and no amount of cursing or fussing was going to stop me from playing soccer with my friends in the field. When my aunt would visit he would caution her to keep an eye on me and not allow me to go to the field to play. She tried her best to keep his order but even after a beating she couldn't stop me. I told her it was pointless to punish me because I had no plans on staying in the house. She could beat me every day if she wanted, but I was still going to play soccer. Eventually, she stopped trying and I won the battle.

After a few years with my brother I had a serious secret that only my mother, my brother and I shared. She had never stopped working to get me sent over to her in America and finally it was my time. All of the immigration paperwork had been completed and my paperwork was ready to be processed. My mother came to America in 1991 on a little boat and even in her fear and uncertainty she was determined to bring me to the land of opportunity. I remember when I was a young boy my uncles picked me up from my aunt's house in the countryside. It was a little awkward for me to be with her but it was only for a few days and I was too young to have any expectations of her. There were times when I wondered if she'd forgotten me but I never doubted that she loved me once I was older. The papers had been filed for years and it was just a matter of when I'd get to go with her as she had planned. Even though she didn't live in Haiti she still cared for me when I was with my brother. I couldn't tell my friends or any teacher that I was about to leave the country. It was one of the first things my mother told me and the clerk at the immigration office as well when I went for the first time. They made it seem like I wouldn't be able to go to America if I told anyone what was in the works so I kept my lips sealed.

I was ready to go so it was easy for me to check out at school, I would sleep in class and I no longer cared about passing. Of course when my brother found out about this he scolded me and told me to focus because it would all matter when I came to America. I straightened up a bit. My heart and mind were checked out and no longer in Haiti even though my body was still there. The need to leave was overwhelming at times because life overall is much different in a third world country. The possibility of better can often seem like a pointless wish until you have someone who cares enough to jump through all of the hoops and help you on a date to actually leave. I no longer felt safe in my home with my brother and family and I needed to escape.

One of the most memorable incidents that changed my heart happened a little before my immigration appointment. My father became very sick and we received a call from one of his friends around 8pm. He told us that my dad caught the bus to get to the hospital and a friend of his ended up being at the same hospital and saw him waiting after being treated. Of course the friend offered my dad a ride and even after declining three times the friend wouldn't leave so my father finally accepted the ride. He was riding with his friends after being seen. They pulled away from the hospital and after only driving a few blocks they were pulled over by the police. The vehicle ended up being searched and the findings landed my father in jail along with the friend who was driving.

When we received this call, and after hearing this information, my siblings who lived in the house began to panic and their true character came shining through. One of my sisters even said that because my name was different from theirs they would sell the house that we lived in and divide the money. They thought my dad was going to go to prison and all kinds of discussions and plans were being made. My sister wanted to divide all the money among the children that had my father's last name which meant I would get nothing. Hearing this caused a panic inside, and I felt as if the room was closing in on me. I went outside to catch my breath and sat alone on the steps. As tears filled my eyes my brother came out and put his hand on the back of my neck and said to me, "You know I've always got you." I allowed one tear to escape into my hands as they covered my face. His words provided comfort and let me know that no matter what happened with Dad, I would be ok. I moved my hands from my face and looked up at him, and this time I didn't hide my tears. With every ounce of emotion in my body I said,

"I will do whatever it takes, I just don't want anything to happen to Dad's property. I may not have his last name but I want all of us to stay together." We sat there and talked for a while, and we made a plan to scrape together everything we had if it ever came down to it. That day built our bond even stronger.

Luckily after three months in jail, my father was cleared of all charges and he didn't go to prison but I never felt safe in that house again. I knew my brother was my only ally and my mother had my best interest at heart. She sent money to care for me and the other siblings that weren't her children when my dad was in jail. We never sold the house and my brother still lives there to this day.

Every moment was an opportunity to get stronger or give up. I didn't give up because my brother showed me the power of love and the importance of maximizing every single moment given to me. The day I packed my bag to move to America was the second time in my life that I felt a deep excitement that was laced with nervousness and uncertainty.

Just like my move from the capital to the countryside, I had no idea what was ahead but I wouldn't waste a moment.

"Every moment was an opportunity to get stronger or give up. I didn't give up because my brother showed me the power of love and the importance of maximizing every single moment given to me."

3
KEYS TO THE WORLD

May 22, 2001

After the final hugs passed between my brother and me, I walked into the immigration office at the airport in Haiti. One of the officials at the office gave me a yellow envelope and told me to guard it with my life. They said if it was raining to put it under my shirt and ensure that it stayed dry. Everything seemed to move so fast and every adult who spoke to me was so serious. My original flight was scheduled for 8am and the flight was less than two hours.

As we all boarded the flight, and after getting settled in with my seatbelt fastened, my heart pumped with adrenaline. This was the first plane I'd ever taken so I had no idea what to expect when the pilot's voice came on the speaker. He announced that the plane was experiencing engine failure and we would all have to unload and catch a new plane to America. Of course it would have been too easy for things to go without a hitch. I stayed at the airport for hours waiting for the next flight. Panic set in for a moment as I walked up to the counter to speak with the booking agents at the counter. I knew I needed to gain allies so I could get to America and made it my business to be well behaved and kind as I asked for help. One of the agents returned the kindness by saying, "You are a good kid and you aren't complaining like some of the adults. I will help you get to

America but you will have to wait a while."

I nodded and took a seat in the waiting area by the boarding gate. Time seemed to move at a turtle's pace and many times I wondered if I had been forgotten about. In the moments when the anticipation seemed to be overtaking me the boarding agent would make eye contact. I found solace in her.

When I arrived at the airport in Miami, Florida, I spoke no English but could hear the immigration officer call my name. He said next and pointed a finger for me to come, and I could feel my heart racing and the unfamiliarity didn't ease my anxiety at the time. We went into a small office area and he told me to sign my name on the highlighted lines. I followed his instructions even though I had no clue what I was signing. All I knew for sure was that I was in America and both of my parents seemed to believe I would be better off here so it was the land of fulfilling my desires.

While I sat outside waiting for my parents to pick me up I looked around and said to myself, *I am here, what next?* I don't ever recall feeling as anxious as I did on that day when I arrived in America. I'd taken a journey that many Haitians back home yearned for and this was one one of the greatest opportunities to transform my destiny. It didn't matter that I barely spoke English or came from an unwed teen mom. It didn't matter that I worked in a field or slept in bushes to stay safe in the countryside. At that moment as I sat on a warm bench outside the airport, the most important thing was the next move I was going to make in America! Time seemed to stand still as I took in my new surroundings and before I could ponder any longer on my next moves, my mother arrived.

We lived two hours away from the Miami airport and on the drive home my parents talked to me about America. The most important thing they said to me was, "Now you are here and the only thing we want from you is for you to better yourself. That is why we brought you here." My mother looked at me with a seriousness in her eyes and said, "Do not be like me, I want you to be somebody. The only way you will make it here is through education and once you do, the world is yours!" I sat quietly, replaying the words in my mind. My parents had given me the chance to be a better person and have the best life I could. They hadn't forgotten me as I often thought they did when I lived in the countryside with my aunt. They had a plan for me that took them many years to achieve but they never stopped working on it and that was what mattered the most.

The next morning I woke up at four in the morning to the sound of my mother trying to get ready for work in the dark so she wouldn't wake me. She came over to the bed once she saw I was awake and told me where everything was. She made sure I knew this was now my home and I could help myself to the food and toiletries as I needed to. It felt like she was gone forever and when she finally arrived back home that afternoon I could see the exhaustion on her face. I could see that she was sweaty from the walk and tired from work, and the sight brought tears to my eyes. In my mind I began to replay her words and understood what she was saying. It was on my second day in America that I made my own plan internally to be somebody. It didn't matter how many obstacles I would encounter. I needed to get an education and become somebody so I could help my mother. They gave me life and keys to the world, and I vowed to myself that I would one day repay them with my success.

My first day of school in America was the total opposite to my first day in the capital with my brother. We lived in a small city in Florida and I attended the only high school in the city, Immokalee High School. The good thing about attendant Immokalee was they were no stranger to Haitian students and already had courses in place for English as a second language (ESOL). On the flip side this also meant that there was nothing special about me being there, and I would have to work hard to stand out and be successful. The night before the first day was nerve wracking. I didn't know what to expect of an American school. How was the food, would I get lost? My older brother was back in Haiti so no one would be waiting at the gate for me here at the end of the day. This was fight or fight time and even if I was afraid I had to wake up and check in at school the next day.

When I arrived at the campus I was amazed at its size.

The school was more than thirty nine thousand acres and houses over one thousand students daily. As a foreigner the size alone was intimidating. I stood at the bus ramp frozen by fear and confused about where to go for check in because all of the signs were in English. Even though I spent most of the summer in the library and in adult ESOL course I couldn't recall anything I had learned at that moment. It was all a blur until someone noticed me and helped me find my way to the office. After a back and forth dialogue with a staff member who spoke French and Creole, I was escorted to the wing for Haitian students who needed to learn English and take the placement test. It felt like a secret dungeon for immigrant teens and I immediately noticed the group of troublemakers and made a note in my mind to stay away. I didn't want to get caught up with the wrong crowd because I couldn't get the image of my mother looking beat down after a day of work. She needed me to make something of myself so I could help her.

I sat in the middle of the room and observed as the instructor spoke to us as if we were incapable of communicating intelligently. When I was asked a question I took my time to think critically before answering, I searched the corners of my mind to recall what I'd been learning and observing. I didn't get every question right but I made every effort to show I was there to learn.

After the first week of school passed I was called into the

office and told I would be starting at tenth grade even though I was nearly eighteen and in Haiti I was a senior. This was one of the most unexpected educational setbacks I had ever experienced. I wasn't used to being in this position because in Haiti I had always thrived academically. I sat in the chair and blinked as hard as I could to hold back the tears. I was going to have to make the best of this because there was no turning back.

Each day after that I made it my business to speak to the administrators and principal whenever I saw them. I sat in the front of the class and never played around with the other Haitian students. I sat with American students at lunch and listened to them talk because I needed to speak better English. I needed to show myself and everyone there that I wasn't just another immigrant wasting time at school. After months of being in the lower level class I went to the office and advocated for myself so I could be moved to a class with more serious students and could learn more. This was no easy task because I had to speak English to state my case and no one was there to correct my broken sentences or help me find the right words.

I must have caught the attention of the principal as he passed by because later that day he called me into his office. It's been nearly two decades since that conversation but I have never forgotten it.

He had a large office with a chalkboard in the corner on the wall. As we made small talk to build rapport he walked over to the board and wrote three things that have become my personal mantra for life- Goal oriented, determined and hard working. After writing them he looked over at me and said, "You are different from the other kids in your class, and you can do anything you decide to do if you put your mind to it." I sat there frozen and confused for a moment before speaking, "Why are you telling me this now?"

He looked over to me and sat in the chair on the other side of the room before responding, "This is my last year being the principal at this school so I want you to know these three things that will help you be successful." Something within me knew this was another key that I needed for a good life in America so I looked over at him and nodded. He stood and extended his hand for me to shake, it was an unspoken agreement and I knew he was going to see to it that I got into a better class. This added even more fuel to my desire to succeed because I had an American in my corner who had the power to help me.

When I moved classes I went into overdrive with academics. And I immersed myself in American culture, I even wore a do rag on my head like some of my American friends in the new class. I remember hiding it when I was at home because I knew my mother would want to know why I was wearing a piece of fabric on my head.

There were times I missed Haiti and being with my older brother. In those times I would play soccer with my Haitian classmates in the field at school. It wasn't as popular in America so the teams were small and only a few of us played. There was a football coach at my school who saw me kick the soccer ball one day and made it his mission to get me to play. Each time I passed the football field on the way to soccer practice, he tried to recruit me because he saw how far I could kick the ball. I had no interest in football because the players spoke English and in soccer the players spoke creole. Playing a new sport would force me to learn new words in English. My young mind saw it as an unnecessary challenge so I declined the coach every time he asked.

One day he saw me walking and the moment we locked eyes I tried to reroute my path. He was faster than me and jokingly grabbed me by the next while saying, "Hey, I want you to try this! Just come over and kick the ball." Of course I was in no position to decline so I followed his lead and that was the first day that I played football.

When I stood on the football field for the first time I could hear the coach yelling, "Kick the ball," but I had no idea what he meant. I stood there puzzled until my Haitian classmate yelled out, "Choute boul la," and I knew to kick it. After that day football quickly became one of my greatest joys and accomplishments. It taught me drive and motivated me to embrace discomfort. My initial fear came from the thought that I would get hurt and the other half was the language barrier.

Both of those obstacles were quickly addressed with education of the proper technique to use to avoid injury and repetition with English words. I said no at least five times before the coach made me join the team but I am glad he did. When I said no to him, I was really saying no to my potential because it came with challenges. Just as the saying goes, "Nothing good comes from our comfort zone."

I applied myself to football because the chances of me getting a scholarship were greater. I didn't like to lose and when given the chance, I always maximized my moment on the field. One example of this is my junior year of high school at the district championship qualifier game. We played against a team that always seemed to win but I had never been on the field with them. My coach had a strong belief in me and looked at me on the sidelines. I saw the fire in his eyes and he saw the determination in mine. Something in that moment reminded me of my brother and I made up my mind that I was going to win the game for him. After that thought filled my mind I paced on the sidelines waiting for my moment and shortly after the coach called my name. "I know you can do it, go kick the ball" The excitement and motivation hugged me tightly as pure adrenaline ran through my veins. I remembered my brother sewing my uniform and teaching me French. I remembered him coming to get me from my aunts and I knew this was my moment to make him proud. I inhaled until my lungs reached their maximum

" When I said no to him, I was really saying no to my potential because it came with challenges. Just as the saying goes, "Nothing good comes from our comfort zone."

capacity and kicked the ball with all the force my body possessed. We won the game in the last five seconds after I kicked a thirty five yard field goal.

That game showed me how precious moments were and the powerful things I could accomplish when I maximized them. We won the district championship against the undefeated team and disqualified them from the playoffs weeks later. The day we won the championship game was memorable on so many levels because I finally felt like I belonged and that being Haitian didn't matter. After the buzzer alerted the crowd of our win everyone rushed to the field and held me high in the air.

When I returned to school on Monday, I was the king! Nothing could bring me down as I floated through the halls. While on my way to class I remember being pulled to a side corner by a girl I liked. We wanted to talk to each other but there was a language barrier that we couldn't seem to get squared away, none of that mattered on this day. Before I could even try to speak she planted a kiss on my lips. I guess she also knew how to maximize a moment! Of course, one of my teammates saw the kiss and it became the joke of the year. I didn't care much because I was the king of the field and the kiss sealed the deal.

Winning on the field was nice but I tried to keep the real goal in my mind. I wanted to win with education so I could succeed in my life. College was the goal and football was a key that could unlock the door to more. I often wonder how my life would have been if that coach hadn't encouraged me to kick the ball that day. I still don't know why he decided to grab my neck and make me try but I'm glad he did.

Winning helped me see that what you do is more important than where you come from. When I was doing my best at school and the principal noticed and helped me, it didn't matter that I came from Haiti. When I helped win the championship game, it didn't matter that I didn't always speak clear English.

The only thing that matters is what you do with each opportunity you are given. I was always good enough but I didn't know it until I stretched myself beyond my comfort zone.

I truly became enough when I believed being Haitian never held me back!

"I truly became enough when I believed being Haitian never held me back!"

4
ALL EYES ON ME

Even through my high school setbacks and victories I stayed focused on academics and presevered because my ultimate goal was going to college. After a brief conversation with one of the high school administrators I found out about a program that allowed immigrant high school seniors pick three schools, and be admitted to one. My choices were University of Miami, University of South Central Florida, and University of South Florida in Tampa. I picked University of Miami first because it was where I studied for my English comprehensive assessment required by the state of Florida (FCAT). Over the summer before my senior year I received tutoring and test preparation assistance because I had to pass the FCAT to graduate. After spending the whole summer there I had an idea about college.

During my first semester as a senior several colleges visited the high school campus. I saw a student go in to talk with them but I didn't really understand at first because a few of the teachers were discouraging foreign kids. I had to take initiative and push past the discouragement and being left out of important conversations, reviewing options and next steps for college. I recall anxiously glancing over at the table where one of the recruiters was sitting, while thinking let me give this a shot. After taking a deep breath and regaining my confidence I walked over to greet a guy from the Edward Waters College table. I picked up one of the pamphlets as one of the yearbooks for the school caught my eye. Something within me was interested and I wanted to know more about this school. To this day I cannot explain why I felt the instant connection after lightly brushing my hand across the yearbook. Looking back at it I believe it was a divine moment that helped me make one of the best decisions of my life.

I opened the pamphlet and instantly saw that it was a very small campus, which caused me to relax a little because I came from a small town. Even though I had my top three choices in mind already, that one interaction caused me to apply to Edward Waters College. I started the application process that night when I arrived home. I knew I would get admitted to one of the other top schools I selected but in my heart I had already chosen Edwards Waters. Plus they had a football team that I had done a trial for and I made it onto the team.

When my high school graduation day arrived, I couldn't contain the joy I felt inside as I reflected on my accomplishment. Getting an American high school diploma was one of the keys I needed to fulfill my life's goals. My eyes filled with tears as I remembered some of my classmates that used to help me throughout my time in high school. My brother in Haiti came to mind as I thought of the two brothers who helped me with my homework and pretty much anything else I needed. They called themselves the Brown Boys and we eventually became best friends and one of them used to cut my hair. Wherever you saw them I was usually close by even in the classroom. Our seats were always close and we did what we could for each other to make sure we all passed the FCAT.

We went into the class on test day with a plan and the brother sitting behind me knew to pay attention to my test because I had told him I would move slow so he could see some of my answers. I was devastated when I found out that he failed by only two points and couldn't get a diploma, but he received a certificate of completion instead. On graduation day his brother sat next to me on my right while he sat on my left with his head down the whole time. At that moment I wasn't thinking about my accomplishment, but instead I was thinking about him. I had a total of seven friends in high school who didn't receive a high school diploma on that day.

I snapped out of my sadness just as the teacher signaled for my row to stand and walk toward the stage. It finally clicked in my head that this was really happening as they called my name to shake the principal, former principal and superintendent's hand. I smiled as I shook their hands and when I arrived in front of the former principal, he handed me my diploma and tapped my shoulder three times saying, "I knew you would be successful." When I sat back down in my seat I felt a sense of pride and confidence because I could move forward with my life. When I looked over into the crowd and saw my family, I couldn't hold back my smile. My uncles were there, and they gave me money and all kinds of stuff. I appreciated their support and love on that day. Deep down I knew that if it wasn't for their dedication and the support from the teachers, principal and all the other staff members believing in me, I would never have graduated. Even the ones who made fun of me acknowledged me on graduation day. One particular person comes to mind, a guy named Mr. Medina. He was the person over the program when I used to play football.

He would say, "Man you the waterboy, you don't even know what to call a play." Then he followed up with, "But you have the drive, and you are going to make it." After graduation he walked over to me as I stood with my family and gave me an envelope with fifty dollars while saying, "You are the waterboy." When I opened the card he wrote a note inside that said you are going to be successful because you have the drive.

The principal and football program leader's words rang in my mind so I was determined to win no matter what. A few weeks later I received my official acceptance package in the mail. I nervously tore open the letter with the Edward Waters College seal and my heart felt as if it would beat out of my chest. I don't think I slept for two days because I was so proud of myself and happy that I was really going to college.

I talked to different people whose opinion I valued and shared the final news with my parents and other family members. My mom was happy for me to go to college but my dad wasn't happy about the choice of the school that I'd made because the school was a historically black college (HBCU). Many HBCU's are underfunded and don't have as many resources as other non HBCU'S but I didn't care about that. For me it meant something to go to a college that valued me as a minority and would allow me the opportunity to better myself. Edward Waters University is Florida's first HBCU and it remains one of the only private HBCU'S in existence in the state. The university motto is emerging eminence and that alone resonated with me even before I stepped foot on the campus. I noticed the motto as I scanned my acceptance package, carefully taking in every word on the page. It was the first time I had ever heard the word eminence which meant superiority. This word described my journey perfectly! I had emerged from a small town in the countryside of Haiti to become one of the first in my family to obtain a high school diploma in America. Even if I didn't finish college I had already redirected my path and maximized the opportunity my parents provided to me.

As I held the papers in my hands I recalled the plane ride to America and finally understood that a delay wasn't a denial when it was paired with focus, hardwork and determination. I could have grown frustrated when my aunt paid for my cousin to go to school but not me.

I could have become complacent in my thinking and lost the belief in myself to learn. Instead I challenged myself to take a risk and even though I started late, I still got the opportunity to start. I was used to the obstacles and willing to do the work to overcome them.

College would be no different. Just like the motto I planned to emerge eminently!

August 13th, 2004

Things started off a little rocky when my father pulled up to the college to drop me off and get me unpacked at the dorm. I could see my father clutching the steering wheel as we drove up and saw a bunch of students sitting outside smoking weed. At first glance I wanted to believe it was just a cigarette but once we opened the car door there was no denying what it was because the smell of weed filled the outside air. It angered my father so much that he decided not to go inside, and he looked over at me with cold eyes and informed me that he wasn't going inside this dump because he thought I would be one of those guys after a few weeks. I just shook my head but I didn't say anything aloud. He wasn't happy with the whole thing. This was a new response because he had been okay with the school on our first visit. I didn't like the sight either but I knew at that time I had a choice to make. The choice wasn't about what people would think about me, it was always about what *I* thought about me. I made up my mind and kept saying I'm not going to fail. I tucked my father's words in the corner of my mind and they would become one of the things to keep me going.

My mother walked over to the car as I opened the door and began unloading my things. She gave me a weak smile and that was enough to reinvigorate my excitement. I had already surpassed the educational accomplishments of my father and while his words hurt I knew I still had someone in my corner. Mom didn't say anything about the weed smokers loitering outside; she simply picked up a bag and followed me into the dorm to help me unpack. She unpacked all my stuff, fixed my bed and made sure I knew how much she loved me with a tight motherly hug. And then they left without my dad ever going inside to see where I would be living. Discouragement seemed to sit on the bed next to me after my mother pulled away from the parking lot that day. The only thing that kept me going was speaking positively in my mind to myself. I stood up and looked around, thinking I'm going to make it regardless. I'm not going to give up. I'm going to get up in the morning and do what I need to do.

The next morning, I woke up and made my way to the cafeteria where I faced my first challenge, adapting to American traditions and culture. In Haitian culture we barely ate breakfast so when I walked into the cafeteria, I couldn't find any of the food I was accustomed to having. The admission director, Tony Baldwin saw me sitting alone with a look of stress and anxiety as I began to feel homesick. The cafeteria was upstairs, and I sat alone near the window looking down at the cars that were passing by. He quietly walked up behind me and put his hand on my shoulder before saying, "Young man, what's going on with you?"

Without turning around to look him in the eyes I just shook my head and weakly whispered. "I'm okay."

He responded with a gentle assertiveness, "No, you're not okay. I know you're not. I saw your parents leaving yesterday and noticed that your father left after you unpacked the car alone." The feelings of discouragement seemed to be rising with each word he spoke but I couldn't allow the emotions to overtake me in the cafeteria, so I blinked back the tears and listened to his words.

He said, "You are a good kid, but I sense that something is bothering you. What is in your mind?"

I cleared my throat and replied flatly, "I wanna go home."

"Why do you want to go home already, it's just the first day?" He responded with palatable concern before I could even finish the sentence.

I paused for a moment taken aback by his interest at the moment.

"I just wanna go home. I can't find any food to eat, and I don't know anyone." It was as if someone had poked an emotional balloon to let all the air out inside me. This moment was different because no family member was coming to save me. My brother was back in Haiti and my parents were back at their homes in another city. This was my battle to fight and there I was helplessly sitting on a cafeteria bench sulking about not being able to find any food to eat.

Tony never missed a beat and the moment I ended my sentence he began to speak, "Well, we have plenty of food here for you to choose from, let's start there." As he gestured to me, I followed him over to food and he taught me how to make cheese grits. He patiently demonstrated how to put salt and then cheese in it and then heat it up, so the food is hot. He must have sensed my curiosity as I wondered how he knew this would be something I liked. Before I could ask, he looked at me and said, "There's a lot of Haitian kids here on campus who like this and they would probably make it for you but I want to show you how you can help yourself."

I nodded my head in understanding and returned to my seat to eat my breakfast. He became my first ally and that became my breakfast every morning.

My freshman year seemed to go by without any major incidents other than my decision to not play football so I could focus on education. Initially, I intended to major in theology because in my mind I would try to be a pastor. The same chairperson of the criminal justice department was also a professor for the theology program. When I was in Haiti, I was Catholic and at one point I desired to be one of the Catholic priests. So, I paid close attention to the teachings and read a lot of stuff in the Bible. The way she was teaching it was wrong, so we kept bumping heads, because I was the type of person that if something wasn't right, I was gonna tell you it wasn't right. The final straw was during the Bible 101 course when I questioned something she was teaching. Of course, she pushed back and told me that if I wanted to pass in this program with this major, I needed to stop being difficult because she taught seven courses in that degree. There was no getting away from her, but I didn't want it to impact my happiness at the university or my faith. The next day I changed my major to criminal justice because I wanted to make a difference and do something impactful. I would still have to deal with the professor but this time it wasn't not difficult because she would be teaching me something new. Sometimes you have to play the game to get to the end goal. Working in the fields of Haiti taught me that!

As I settled into my new major, I made a few friends and connections but there was an unexplainable longing within me to do more than just attend and graduate. As fate would have it, the opportunity to do more quickly arose. One morning as I sat in the dorm area, I noticed the newspaper headlines with our school's name in bold letters. The article explained how a freshman was shot the day after he wrote an essay criticizing campus safety. Before getting shot the student was standing outside of his dorm when he was approached by two men who demanded his sports jersey, cell phone and wallet. This led to him

" Sometimes you have to play the game to get to the end goal. Working in the fields of Haiti taught me that! "

writing and submitting the essay on how he felt unsafe on campus. Something inside of me felt connected to his story and saddened by the fatal shooting that could have possibly been avoided. I quickly gathered my things and went to the computer lab and started doing research on the issue of safety at the campus.

My major was criminal justice, so I felt obligated to do something. We deserved to feel safe at school even if it was located in the hood. There were always a lot of questionable things going on in the neighborhood and sometimes it was hard to identify who was a student because of the lack of security on campus. Oftentimes I saw the Jacksonville sheriff office keep passing by on the street every day but they never stopped on campus. I'd heard different stories about campus safety issues but no real solution seemed to be in the works. About a month after reading the article and researching the issue I noticed a flier from the department chair requesting a meeting with every student who majored in criminal justice. They wanted to meet with all of us to discuss creating a criminal justice club.

After we decided that this was something we wanted to do, the next step was to appoint a club president. I was still a freshman at the time, and I wasn't as vocal as I had been in high school. This was also a new process for me because I didn't join any clubs in high school. As I sat observing the process frustration began to rise because none of the upperclassmen volunteered to take on the role of president. One of the professors present at the meeting asked about three times for volunteers but nobody did anything. After the third round of silence I waved my hand and surprised myself with my bold declaration, "I will."

A few of the freshman and sophomore girls nearby objected, saying, "Nobody can even hear you talking. You have a heavy accent. You can't even speak English properly, and now you wanna be the criminal justice club president?"

The embarrassment I felt gripped me like a tight hug. No one else was volunteering so I stepped up and I felt like I had received a slap in the face and wanted to crawl underneath the seat and hide. The department chair stood in the front of the room with a stern face and said, "If anyone here has a mouth to speak, regardless of what you say, at some point somebody will understand the message no matter the language or accent."

I felt like he was really standing up for me as he went on to explain how my efforts to learn American language and cultures set me apart from them. They all seemed to understand when he painted a clear picture of how I could speak three languages while they could only speak one. My accent was strong but I had the ability to reach more people because I could speak more languages. The situation in the room instantly shifted in my favor and everyone was in agreement with me becoming the club president.

I started taking the lead and doing more to assert my voice because everyone was under me in the club. As the president I worked closely with the department chair and other members of leadership in the school. I kept the fatal shooting and campus safety in mind and decided I needed to start a new program that could tackle the issue of campus safety. I did research to see what different programs they had in the city with the Jacksonville sheriff office and came across a program called Sheriff Advising Counseling (SHACO). I didn't send the information to anyone else or wait to talk with the chair who spoke clear English without an accent. Instead, I picked up the phone and called the sheriff myself. He wasn't in the office at the time I called so I left my information. The receptionist on the other end didn't provide any hope and ended the call by saying, "Okay, well if it's important enough they will call you." I believed it was important enough especially with the recent headlines about the fatal shooting. Two days later the sheriff called me.

"Hello, this is Sheriff John Rutherford, I got your message and wanted to follow up with you on this. What's your name and student ID number?" When I heard his name and voice on the other end my heart began to race. I sat straight up in my chair and spoke as confidently and clearly as possible as I answered his questions. After confirming my information, I expressed my concern for safety as my mind raced before asking for what I truly wanted to accomplish. Luckily the sheriff asked me what I thought could be done and then I asked if they could do the program on campus. There was a moment of silence that caused me to hold my breath in anticipation. I filled the silence by telling him that I was also the President of the criminal justice club and the goal was to put things in place where we could have more access to the law enforcement at least when we needed stuff.

His response surprised me and made me feel like he agreed with the urgency and the need to turn things around with campus safety. "Okay. I'm coming to meet with you on campus. What day is best for you?"

I could tell he was serious and invested in what I was saying so I replied quickly and enthusiastically, "I am available on the second Thursday of the month."

We confirmed a time, and I ran over to the chairman's office to share the news. As I spoke with him, I couldn't help but recall the girls who laughed at my accent. The sheriff fully understood me, my voice mattered!

The support I received from the police and school leadership was unexplainable. All I could think about was the day my father dropped me off and said I would become like the boys he saw standing in front of the building smoking weed. I wasn't like them, I was making a difference and my choice to attend an HBCU was working in my favor. The program started shortly after the initial meeting with the sheriff and the same girls who laughed were now asking me how I was able to achieve such a large goal in a short amount of time.

After hiding in abandoned buses and trees back in Haiti I knew the value of a safe environment. Being in college and making a difference gave me confidence that wasn't connected to my performance on the football team. When I think about it now I can see how many people struggle with finding their place in college because they ignore the small things that point them to their path of purpose and fulfillment.

What if I would have ignored the tug in my heart to attend Edward Waters or allowed my father's words to make me withdraw my decision? What if I had never seen the newspaper and paid attention to the urge to do something? I now know that stepping onto that campus and unloading that car was my first adult decision.

It was me taking charge of my life and using the key to the world that my parents gave me when they brought me to America.

I unlocked my voice when I stopped allowing the opinions of others to determine my outcome. I was going to keep speaking even if no one listened but judging from my results, all eyes and ears were on me.

" I unlocked my voice
when I stopped
allowing the opinions
of others to determine
my outcome. "

5

LIMITLESS

"If you want to be an elite, you have to put aside the limitations in your mind." -Tim Grover

Once I began to see all the things I could accomplish by using my voice and taking initiative, I became a leader on campus. There was an unquenchable thirst within me to keep going and make sure that no other student was fatally shot while I was a student at the university. The sheriff's office provided a police figure on campus every day when we had class. After that I made sure I maximized every opportunity to use my voice with the Sheriff.

As my sophomore year came to a close I settled into the power of my influence on campus and decided I wanted to deepen the impact. Just like many other times in my life I had to make the choice to act on my intuitions I felt. I knew we needed more than just the police presence; we needed to create a space for the officers to be there even outside of class time. With this in mind I approached the sheriff one day as I saw him sitting in his car on campus. I casually mentioned the idea of them having a substation on our campus since we definitely had the space. I could see the gears in his mind turning as he processed the idea. If they had a station on campus there would always be a police car or extra security to deter criminals. It would be a win overall for the campus. He thanked me for the idea and we parted ways. Shortly after that conversation I found out they were developing a substation on campus and that substation remains on the campus today.

My college success showed me that it's okay if others

don't think you know what you are doing. It's only important for you to know and confidently pursue your goal. When I raised my hand to volunteer for club president I didn't know the steps to take. I just knew I had to do something so no other parent or freshman saw what I'd seen. On the first day, the campus looked like an unsafe hangout spot. I remember when I was in Haiti, I never wanted to be a policeman, but I always saw myself in the law enforcement, probably a lawyer, judge or a prosecutor. I'd always wanted to make a difference, but I also didn't see myself in the field walking around and chasing people. Deep down I always saw myself as a problem solver, and I believe that's what caused me to unconsciously raise my hand for the role.

By the time my senior year rolled around I'd received so many awards and certifications from the Jacksonville sheriff's office and the school program for my leadership. The campus was my new home and I was determined to take care of it in a way I hadn't been able to do for my home back in Haiti with my aunt or brother. Once the criminal justice department saw my willingness to take action I participated in several other initiatives, including an important citywide survey to serve Duval County. As an immigrant I made a difference because I could speak to other immigrants and explain the importance of the survey. I also did an internship with Jacksonville Transportation Authority where I helped develop different programs to help them save millions of dollars and improve efficiency.

I thrived in my community work but struggled significantly with the college courses that weren't directly related to criminal justice but I couldn't quit. The community work I was doing in college really gained a reputation back in Haiti, and it was a positive pressure to finish what I started. Sometimes pressure and expectations are good if they help you stay on track. I struggled the most with my humanities class but replaying my father's words made me push myself harder. I didn't want to be a college drop out smoking weed in front of the dorm. The humanities professor reminded me of my father in many ways because there was a high expectation to perform, but there wasn't always much teaching that helped me truly understand the concepts. But I couldn't let that stop me, and once I realized that pretty much everything was repetitive and I would just sit in the class and push myself to make a C to pass. I had to learn how to make my life easier by doing things my way.

In math I did all my homework in the classroom while the teachers were talking and the information was fresh. I was a strong reader because I wanted to know things about the world long before moving to America. College helped me become a confident man who was sure of his strengths, unafraid to use his voice and dedicated to emerging eminently!

The influential men and women I encountered in my life have served a purpose and played a role in my life's movie. They helped me to grow even when it felt like punishment or pain.

Looking back at my life in Haiti I feel an overwhelming gratitude. The good thing about life is, it will always bring you who you need at the exact time you need them but you must be open to receiving their help in the way they can give it. My aunt said yes to raising me and did the best she could at times. Without the experiences in her home I wouldn't have known how to advocate for myself. I wouldn't have developed self determination. I wouldn't have learned survival skills or appreciated the gift of being given an opportunity. As a child she frightened and enraged me because her love didn't look like the vision I had in mind. She passed away on January 2nd, 2022, as I finished the first draft of this book, but her impact will forever remain in my heart. Her passing reminded me to never forget who helped you because no one owes you anything. Without her I wouldn't know how to write my name or read aloud flawlessly. I smile as I write this because I was able to support her financially after graduating college and ensure her burial in Haiti preserved her dignity. She was the first to teach me that everyone leaves you with a lesson that can motivate you to see and do more!

After college graduation I met a man named Greyson Marshall Jr. who helped me see myself in a better way. The way you see yourself matters and it helps to have good people around to help you see the best you and be better. Immediately after graduating college, I did things just to do them, without a purpose. Life felt purposeless because I'd accomplished all of my educational goals, but I had no idea what to do after completion. I had drive, but no clear vision or direction. Having drive is good but without a clear vision you will aim at every target hoping to find gold. Internal visioning is the key to external accomplishments. When I saw myself better inside it improved my perspective on the encounters I had with others. One of the most important relationships we have is our personal relationship with ourselves. When you work on yourself you become untouchable because you achieve goals you set and carry out your purpose. There is value in who you are, and it matters how you see yourself because you set your price!

I took a job that paid well and I seemed to thrive but I knew I could be in management. That became my next goal and I worked hard to stand out among coworkers and finally the day arrived when I was ready to approach my manager about a higher level role. He agreed that I was a great asset to the company, then told me that my accent was my only barrier to advancement. I replayed the limiting words of my former supervisor like a broken record in my mind, "Franky, you meet the qualifications, but you have a diction problem." That brought my spirit down because I knew I could do the job. I told him I wouldn't give up and I believed in myself fiercely. I moved from the fifth best seller to number 1 for nine months in a row trying to prove my worth. I was even enrolled in all of the top programs at the company and thrived, but I never got the promotion. I knew that many people with my same accent had overcome obstacles like this one. It was frustrating because for the second time in my life someone was telling me that my voice wasn't good enough to lead others. I remember feeling defeated walking out of that office but I remembered the words of my former principal and coach. They fed into my unbreakable spirit and determination to win, so I wasn't going to let them down by quitting now. In moments of frustration I tapped into the words from people who fed good things into me. As a result of his doubts, I currently hold a management position.

To get into my current position I created a 90 day greatness plan for myself. I knew it was up to me to transform my life and professional achievements. I set out to become a manager and for 30 days I told at least one person about my plan. I would be assisting people who came into my job with such greatness and when they complimented me I responded with " I am going to be manager soon" My coworkers would question my initiative at moments when I went above and beyond but I did not care. I would smile and reply with my plan to be a manager one day. I tapped into my deep burning desire to rise above the circumstances.

After the first 30 days I looked back over my first thirty days and all the mistakes I made. I looked at the mistakes closely and dissected the lessons from them. This was a vital part of my growth because all I did for fifteen days was look at one mistake or hangup I made and write down the lessons. There was much discouragement during the fifteen days of evaluation. I watched people less qualified than me advance while others quit or got fired. I listened to the laughs of those who did not believe a Haitian man with a strong accent could be a leader in an American company that relied on clear communication and speech. Once I arrived at day 45 I felt reinvigorated because I was laser focused on my target.

When we have laser focus on a goal or plan we can apply the lessons we have learned from our past hang ups and mistakes. Days forty-five through sixty seemed to roll by with ease because I found my rhythm. There were three things I kept in my mind each day: understand the lesson, apply the remedy and evaluate your progress. I started waking up early to go to the gym and listened to books that helped me keep growing as I transformed. Even when I saw no progress, I stayed committed because I needed to see the end result of applying myself to something with full energy for 90 days.

By the time day sixty rolled around I knew for sure what I was working for and had a clear vision on how to get there. I took every training offered and if anyone needed a day off they called me. I showed up with gladness because every day got me closer to my transformation from employee to manager. I kept my 90 day greatness plan on repeat for nine straight months with no breaks. I went from fifth on the top seller list to the number one top seller. By the end of the third 90 days, I was untouchable and applied for the management role again. The manager who told me I could not advance because of my accent lit a fire within me to fully transform into the greatest and most focused version of myself.

So many people come into our life and some come for good, while others come for a different reason. But you have to look at each one of them as they will be a lesson that will make you grow. Even the bad things can help motivate you to gain more, and possibly see a different version of yourself in a place you could have never imagined. This perspective had kept me in a place of continuous gratitude. I could still hold bitterness in my heart about my mom giving me up when I was a baby. I could be mad about going to my dad's family and the treatment from my aunt. But what I now know is that was probably the better way to handle things. I say this because at the end of the day, they still helped me to grow and get to where I want to be. Without my aunt I would not know how to read. Her methods were awkward but effective and if she had not given me the chance to go to school I would not be here today. Holding onto hurt would have placed limits on my growth and in no way could it have helped me get to where I am today. The friendship, relationship, really anybody that comes to your life, they come to your life for a reason and they come into your life to teach you something.

The second most important relationship you can have is

with others. One relationship with my mentor Grayson Marshall Jr. helped me see myself as more than just a Haitian man in America trying to make it. He helped me to see the best version of myself and to understand how to redefine myself to the person that I am today. When I met him, I was lost and aimlessly stumbling through each day. I went to work out of habit with no real plans or dreams until he showed me tough love. He's the guy that tells you what you need to hear, not what you want to hear, and sometimes that's a hard pill to swallow. The greatest lesson he taught me was that the past only matters if you do something with it. He always told me that my struggle could be an asset if I worked on my thinking to see myself as more than the struggle. When I met him I felt gratitude instantly because after just one conversation my mind was opening to all the possibilities of who I could be. If I would have approached him with pride I would have missed the lessons he'd taught me. I encourage you to get a mentor that you can learn from and be humble enough to learn. Approach each new relationship and even your existing ones with gratitude. Most of all, find someone who will help you be great even if their delivery is different than yours, and it will challenge you to release your limitations!

You can complete anything you desire to do in life if you BELIEVE in yourself and know that it can really happen. It starts with releasing your limitations and how you use your setbacks. Setbacks will come but you cannot let them hold you back. I had to release the limitation that was placed on me when I started my career. I cannot change my accent, but I can outwork and release anyone who tries to limit me because of it. I am now managing in the same industry that he said I wouldn't make it in because of my accent. You could easily give up but what good would that do you in your life?

Look at your life at this moment and ask yourself, "What have I accomplished?" If you don't feel happy with your accomplishments, get to work. Don't allow anything you are experiencing to limit you. Giving up is not an option when it comes to your life. If you want to get ahead, you must change the way you think. It's up to you to do something about your life!

If you want money, speak it and work for it. If you want good health do the work because nothing just happens. We all have 86,400 seconds, each day it is up to you to do something with them. When I started going to the gym each morning and feeding my mind with motivation and knowledge my life transformed. The circumstances were the same but my outlook was brighter because I no longer doubted the power within my unique fingerprint. Once you start changing the way you think and act, everything in your life is going to change. I had to repeat my 90 day plan for nine straight months to become a top seller and get the promotion. I have done it countless times since then but all the results were not the same. I did not win every time but I did transform into a better me. I reached my management goal because I released my mental limitations and allowed myself to use my experiences to help me be the best me. I went from assistant manager to assistant manager and top seller and now I am the branch manager. I am able to speak to people from all backgrounds and use my knowledge of three languages as an asset for the company. The same accent that once was a limitation is now seen as a huge benefit that comes with extra pay. If I would have stopped when someone who only speaks one language discouraged me I would have never made it this far. Use every experience for your good and remember your past experiences are an asset, not a limitation. Your greatness is deep within you waiting to be awakened when you transform into your best self!

" Don't allow anything you are experiencing to limit you. Giving up is not an option when it comes to your life."

90 Day Greatness Plan

Before making a major decision in life, most people put a plan in place to help them achieve it. This is true in life, and we see it often at work. When we start a new job, it is often accompanied by a ninety-day probation period. During that time, we are given job descriptions to master and daily task to execute. Each day we are there for the first ninety days we work hard to achieve the role of permanent employee. Once it's done, we have ongoing evaluations to monitor our progress, but we do not do this same practice in our personal life.

Most people who give themselves a new year resolution never accomplish them because they wait for the new year to start working on themselves. They could easily reset their mindset and start working on my new year resolution three months before the new year comes. This would increase their chances of achieving and maintaining their goal. For example, if you are planning on losing weight there is no way you can lose weight within a short time working out. You will need at least three months to start seeing your body shift in the direction that you plan on working for. In September of 2022 I did my yearly physically and weighed 139lbs, I told myself before I finish writing this book, I needed to be at 145lbs. As we wrap up the final edits on the book on February 28, 2023, I weight 153lbs. I would have never accomplished my weight goal if I did not follow the 90 days plan.

Using the ninety-day plan can help you shift your mind to a different direction in life. I know sometimes things can be difficult to accomplish, but you can simply change something negative into something positive you will see the best version of the outcome.

Use the following plan at any time in your greatness journey and remember, Great things take time!

Days 1-30: SPEAK UP

Talk about your plan every day for 30 days even if it is just for a minute. Start on day one by clearly writing out your plan and sharing with at least one person. This will help you stay accountable to the 90 days of transformation. Be sure to keep a list of the things you say or plan to say about your plan and be very intentional for the first 30 days. Only say what you desire to see and only share your plans or ideas with people who can assist in the development or execution of your plan.

Days 30-45: EMBRACE THE MISTAKES

During this time your excitement may go up and down and you may even make a few mistakes or hang ups as you are building on your plan. The goal is to write down all the mistakes you encounter for 15 days. After reviewing them on day 45, you will have a better understanding of what you have learned. With a better understanding you can determine if the plan is good as it is or if improvements should be made. This time of embracing is important because that's the time that you know for a fact how much patience you are willing to put into it. If you put 30- 45 days into something, you're not gonna give up easily, something within will arise and you will want to keep going a little while longer.

Day 45- 60: UNDERSTAND, APPLY, EVALUATE

The next phase of the plan is all about applying your understanding of the previous lessons and continuous evaluation. You must evaluate each day and every decision you make that can impact your plan. Doing this will help you grow and transform from an underdeveloped plan to a developed and tested plan.

Days 60- 90: ESTABLISHED & TRANSFORMED

At day 60, you finally understand the plan and have the fuel to continue working. If you make it to the end your vision has officially been established. At the end of your first 90 days, your transformation doesn't stop, it just begins. Continue learning from day one and strive to be great at whatever you do.

The 90 day greatness plan can be repeated as many times as you need until you decide to fire yourself or leave your employer.

ABOUT THE AUTHOR

Francky Jeanty was born and raised in Haiti. By the age of 17, he came to the United States to live with his mother and father in a little town called Immokalee Florida. An unpredictably witty, charming, intelligent and challenging young man is how his friends and family describe him. Growing up in Immokalee Florida, Francky always knew that he was going to make something of himself one day; he vowed that he was not going to follow in his parents' footsteps. At the age of 17, he was put in the 10th grade because of a language barrier but that didn't stop him from accomplishing his goals. He was made fun of by his classmates because he didn't understand a word of English. Instead of getting mad and shutting down from the world he looked at it in a positive way and pushed himself to become who he is today.

Someone told him that he would struggle in life because of his accent; again that didn't stop him from accomplishing what he had set out to do and that was to become the best that he could be in life. Francky is a thirty nine year old man that is motivated by the love for learning and succeeding as he strives to become an outstanding person in his community and that's why he decided to create seven second consulting, LCC to motivate kids to get an education. Francky believes that education is the key to success. One of his favorite quotes is, "No condition is permanent as long as you are willing to change your mindset and today he is living that quote. Another favorite quote is, ""I truly become enough when I believe being a Haitian never held me back.

Francky is:

- The Founder and CEO of 7 Second College Consulting, LCC
- Former admissions counselor at Keiser University
- Former admission counselor at Edward Waters College
- Studied criminal justice at Edward Waters College
- Currently: Studied administrative justice at Bellevue University

Today Francky Jeanty is currently living in Jacksonville Florida. He also found the time to mentor young men and women in the community.